Bi~Curious George

An Unauthorized Parody

Bi-Curious George: An Unauthorized Parody

Copyright 2012 Simonian Enterprises

13-Digit ISBN: 978-1-60433-283-4
10-Digit ISBN: 1-60433-283-2

This book may be ordered by mail from the publisher. Please include $3.99 for postage and handling.
Please support your local bookseller first!

Books published by Cider Mill Press Book Publishers are available at special discounts for bulk purchases in the United States by corporations, institutions, and other organizations. For more information, please contact the publisher.

Cider Mill Press Book Publishers
"Where good books are ready for press"
12 Port Farm Road
Kennebunkport, Maine 04046

Visit us on the Web!
www.cidermillpress.com

Design & Illustrations: Shadday Studios (www.shadday.com)
Typography: Times & Brody

Printed in China
1 2 3 4 5 6 7 8 9 0
First Edition

Bi~Curious George

An Unauthorized Parody

Kennebunkport, Maine

This is George.

He lived in the jungle.

He was a straight little monkey

but always very... curious.

One day George saw a man.

He had on a sassy purple beret.

And George got excited, despite himself.

The man saw George too.

"I'm always in the mood for some

hot monkey love," he thought.

"I would like to take him home with me."

He put his beret on the ground,

and, of course, George couldn't help himself.

He came down from the tree

to verify there was a real designer label

inside the jaunty purple chapeau.

The man had looked so sexy in the beret.

George wanted to be sexy too.

He picked it up and put it on.

He felt gayer already.

The beret still smelled of the man's cologne.

George closed his eyes to bask in

the thick cloud of man stank.

The man picked him up quickly

and popped him into his shoulder bag.

"It's a man-purse," said the man.

George was caught. And a little excited.

The man with the sassy purple beret
put George into a little boat
with a strapping young lad
who rowed them to a big ship.
"Hello, sailor!" thought George.
He was sad to be leaving his home,
but he was still a little... curious.

On the big ship, the man took George
out of his murse.
"Finally," thought George.
"I'm not a fucking Chihuahua."

"George, I was once like you. And now I am here to
help you," said the man. "I am going to take you to
a big club in the city called The Zoo. I have a feeling
you will like it there. A lot. You will also enjoy this
special cruise we are on. Now run along and play.
But don't do anything I wouldn't do!"

George promised to be good.
But it is easy for horny little monkeys to forget.

On the deck he found some
oiled-up men dancing and drinking.
He wondered how they could do
so many of these things called "body shots."
He was very curious.
Finally he HAD to try.
It looked easy. But--

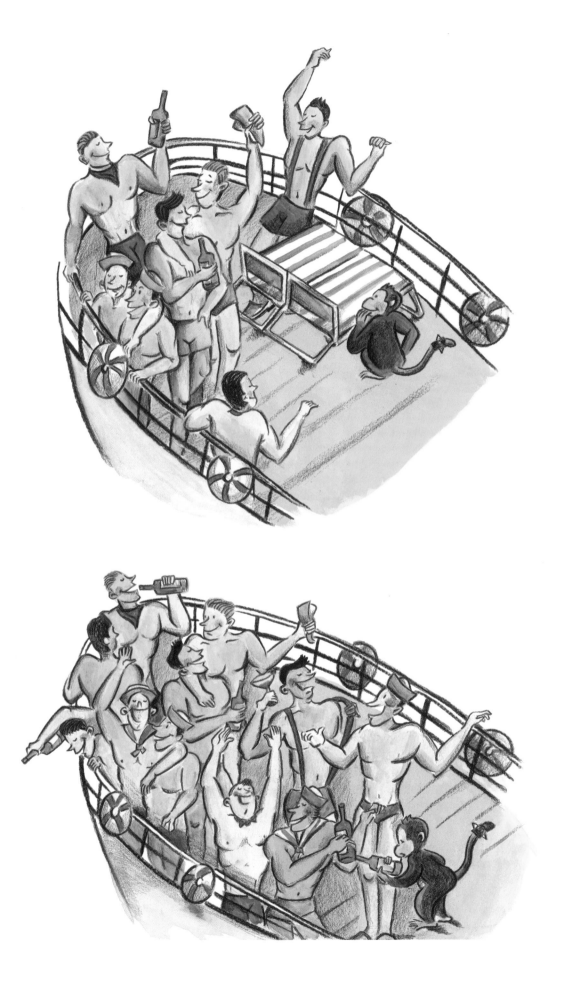

oh, what happened!
First this--

and then this!

"WHERE IS GEORGE?"
yelled every able-bodied seaman.
"Seaman," George giggled between
his dry heaves.
At last they saw him
trying to make himself puke,
and almost all tired out.

"He's on his knees!" cried one sailor.

"But not in a good way!" cried another.

They picked him up. One held his hair,

while the other rubbed his back.

"Best! Night! Ever!" thought George

through all his tears and snot.

And at last he got it all out of his system.

At last, the long trip was over.

"That was the gayest cruise in history,"

thought George.

"You ain't seen nothing yet," said the man.

George and the man with the sassy purple beret

walked down the gangbang--

"GangPLANK," corrected the man--

and on to the man's impeccably decorated

loft in the trendiest part of the city.

After a light vegan supper
and a smoke of something George
quickly realized was not tobacco,
George finally felt relaxed and ready to
make it happen.

He crawled into the man's bed to wait for him.
But the man never came.

So neither did George.

The next morning
George woke up alone and upset.
But you just can't stay angry
with a man who wears the same
purple outfit every day.

The man telephoned The Zoo.
"Whose list are you on?" they asked.
"I'm with the DJ," said the man with
a confident wink and a smile.
George was so turned on.
But the man went away again.

George was lonely.
If the man could find gay love
on the telephone, so could George.
But who to call?
George thought and thought.
Then he started dialing.

DING-A-LING-A-LING!

went the phone at the fire station.

The firemen rushed to the telephone.

"Hello! Hello!" they said.

But George did not answer them.

"Don't worry, we're coming!" they yelled.

"You sure will be!" thought George.

He could picture them racing over and

was so excited. This was the perfect plan.

Firemen were even sexier than sailors!

The firemen rushed through the door.
"WHERE IS THE FIRE?!" they cried.
"In my pants!" George was going to say.
But he stopped himself--
these firemen weren't sexy at all!
They were old and had big bellies.
Where were all the hunky firemen???
George feared that his wall calendars
had been lying to him all these years.

The firemen were very upset that
there was no fire.
"Catch that gay little monkey!" they cried.
"Hey, relax with the labeling!"
thought George as he tried to run away.
He almost made it, but he tripped
over the man's clogs, and---

two firemen grabbed George's arms
and took him to prison.
"You're not even going to use handcuffs?"
thought George. "How disappointing."

George had heard stories about
what happens in prison.
Maybe this wasn't going to be so bad after all.
But they put him in a cell all by himself.
No tatted up cellmates. No group showers.
Prison sucked. George was bummed.

George finally got excited when the gruff
watchman burst into his cell.
But real-life prison guards were even less sexy
than real-life firemen!
George was not interested.
"My first time will not be with THIS guy,"
thought George.
"That would be just embarrassing."
George outsmarted the watchman
and escaped!

Back out in the West Village

George saw a couple of guys buy something

from a man on a street corner.

Whatever it was made them VERY happy.

George was curious.

He felt he MUST have one too.

He reached over and

tried to swipe one for himself, but---

Instead of one tab,
he accidentally took them all!

"I'm going to kill you, you fucking gay monkey!"
cried the drug dealer.

"Hey! I'm just bi-curious!" George
tried to yell as he made his escape.
But it was too late.
George was too far gone.

George felt like he was floating.

Up, up, higher and higher,

way above the city.

The people looked like ants.

And he really wanted to

give them all massages for some reason.

George was frightened and confused.

But he'd never felt freer.

At first, George's trip was awesome.
But then he started coming down.
And he was suddenly very tired.
When he came to, he found
he had climbed a traffic light.
Traffic was all mixed up, and people
were threatening to kick his ass.
"Hate crime!" thought George.

But before he could blow his rape whistle,
he heard someone call,
"GEORGE! YOU SEXY LITTLE BITCH!"
He looked down and saw his friend,
the man with the sassy purple beret!

George was very happy to see the man!
He jumped into his arms,
and the man paid the drug dealer.

"It's a good thing your sugar daddy
has mad cash," said the dealer.
"It sure is," thought George,
snuggling close to the man.

And then George and the man
climbed into the man's yellow Miata
and at last, away they went

to The Zoo!

What a nice place
for George to finally experience
some much needed guy-on-guy action!

About Cider Mill Press Book Publishers

Good ideas ripen with time. From seed to harvest, Cider Mill Press brings fine reading, information, and entertainment together between the covers of its creatively crafted books. Our Cider Mill bears fruit twice a year, publishing a new crop of titles each spring and fall.

Visit us on the Web at
www.cidermillpress.com

or write to us at

12 Port Farm Road
Kennebunkport, Maine 04046